Doggie Tales:
Lessons on Life, Love, and Loss
I Learned From My Dog

Peggy Mitchell Norwood, Ph.D.

livingwell
PRESS.

Denver, CO

Doggie Tales: Lessons on Life, Love, and Loss I Learned From My Dog

Copyright © 2014 Peggy Mitchell Norwood
Published by Living Well Press, LLC
Denver, Colorado
www.LivingWellPress.com

Printed in the United States of America
ISBN-13: 978-0-9817225-2-8

To my friend,
Jacqueline West,
who introduced me to
my sweet little Dallas

CONTENTS

ACKNOWLEDGEMENTS

Thank you to all of you who shared a doggie tale with me and allowed me to tell the story of your furry, four-legged friend.

INTRODUCTION

Yesterday, my sweet dog, Dallas, whom I'd had for only a little more than a year, ran out of the yard, darted across a busy street, and was killed by a car.

I got her in Dallas, Texas in 2006. She had been abandoned by her previous owners when they moved to California. Their neighbor was my friend, Jacqueline West, who took Dallas in when she saw her wandering around the neighborhood. Jacquie already had three dogs of her own, so she was trying to find a permanent home for Dallas when I arrived for a visit.

Impulsively, I blurted out, "I'll take her!" Hearing the words coming out of my mouth surprised even me. A few days later, at the conclusion of my visit with Jacquie, I headed home to Colorado, with Dallas in my lap for the entire 13-hour trip back to Denver.

Never having owned a dog before, I was caught off guard by the way that Dallas stirred something deep inside of me. She was a lot of work in the beginning and remained a challenge until the end, but through it all, I loved her. Not a day went by over the 16 months that Dallas was with us that I didn't tell her, "You're just the cutest little thing, the sweetest little dog in the world."

This book is the story of my time with Dallas and what I learned about God, life, love, and loss. Regardless of what you may be going through or where you are, my prayer is that you will be able to see the hand of God in your life and his abounding love for you. And when all is said and done, know that when life bites, you don't have to bite back.

LESSON ONE

YOU CAN LEARN A LOT ABOUT YOURSELF (AND GOD) FROM A DOG

I must begin with a disclaimer: I am NOT a dog lover nor am I an expert on dogs.

Given the title of this book and the picture of my cute little dog, Dallas, on the cover, this disclaimer might surprise you. How could the author of a book called, *Doggie Tales* not love dogs?

To tell you the truth, I don't really even *like* dogs. I never would have dreamed I'd own a dog. My kids had asked for a dog, and I got them gerbils. But this book is not actually about loving or hating dogs. This book is about how one particular dog came along at just the right time and changed my life.

> *"You can learn a lot about yourself if you have a dog."*
>
> - Nora Vamosi-Nagy
> (a Hungarian dog trainer)

I met Dallas the day after my divorce in June of 2006. The year leading up to my divorce was one of the most painful times of my life. I wrote about it in my book, *Do Something Different…For a Change*. Despite all of the grieving I had done during the year that I was separated, I wasn't prepared for the profound sadness I would experience the day my marriage officially came to an end.

I had decided ahead of time that I wouldn't cry in the courtroom and I held back my tears as the judge pronounced that our marriage was legally dissolved. But if I had it to do over again, I think I would have let the tears flow. The bible says the two shall become one flesh and our one flesh was being torn apart that day. I think that certainly gave me something to cry about.

Torn Asunder

The closest experience I've had to my physical flesh being torn apart was when I was a little girl and I got hit by a taxi while riding my bike. Even though my father had told me to stay on our block and not to go across Powell's Lane, I wanted to play with my friends, so I disobeyed him and crossed over anyway. When I was done playing, I was all set to sneak back home before my father noticed I was gone. The last thing I remember was looking over my shoulder to wave goodbye to my friends. I didn't even see the taxi coming.

I came to on the ground; the front of my bike was smashed and my foot was tangled up in the mangled wheel. My blue canvas sneaker had been ripped open and I had a big gash on my right foot just below my last three toes.

I let out a wail and cried, until out of nowhere, my dad appeared, swooped me up in his arms, comforted me, and carried me home. Little did I know then, that almost 40 years later, my little Dallas would also run across a street in disobedience and get hit by a car.

Yes, if I had to do it over again, I would have let the world (well, the courtroom at least) know just how painful it was for my 14-year marriage to come to an end. I'm not sure why I decided that I wouldn't cry in the courtroom.

Perhaps, I was afraid that if I cried, I'd never stop or that if I opened "the flood gates," there'd be nobody there to rescue me. It wasn't until much later that I learned that if I don't let out a wail and acknowledge my pain, God can't swoop me up in his arms, comfort me, and carry me home.

One For the Road

I decided a road trip would be just the thing to give myself the time and space to feel my pain. I considered my options of whom to visit during this emotionally tumultuous time. Who would be able to offer some measure of comfort, but also know when to leave me alone? Who would listen and empathize with me, but not goad me on? "Girl, be glad you got rid of that man" was *not* what I needed to hear.

I immediately thought of my friend Jacqueline West, whom I knew from my time as a graduate student at the University of Virginia. Jacquie had a calm temperament and now lived in Dallas, Texas. I imagined the day-long drive would be just the thing to clear my head.

Jacquie was a year ahead of me in school. She was married to a chef and lived off campus with him and their dog, Delta. I used to love staying at their house for the weekend, not only because they lived in a small town called Barboursville— the perfect retreat for a stressed out graduate student—but because Jacquie was a great cook herself.

When I visited Jacquie's house, I feasted on southern fried chicken, pork chops, macaroni and cheese, greens, and sweet tea. (Jacquie taught me how to make iced tea using a coffee maker: Run two pots of water over ten tea bags and add one cup of sugar. Perfect sweet tea every time!)

Anticipating seeing Jacquie for the first time in many years made the pain I was feeling just a little more bearable. Jacquie has the kind of laugh that makes you happy. Just hearing her laugh makes you want to laugh, too, even if you missed the joke. How delightfully unexpected that, while visiting this old friend during one of the most painful times in my life, I would meet a new friend who would bring me so much joy!

When I arrived at Jacquie's house, Dallas greeted me warmly. She passed by everyone else, ran straight to me, and jumped up into my lap. She was the perfect lap dog, weighing in at only 7 pounds. I immediately fell in love with Dallas, whose original owners had named her Chai. She was the color of frothy milk with splashes of caramel and had the most adorable face. She was just the sweetest, most affectionate, cutest little dog I had ever met. And so, I took her home with me.

A Reason and a Season

As I look back, it was no coincidence that I met Dallas just one day after my divorce. I believe God brings people and experiences into our lives exactly when they are needed and when we are ready for the lessons they can teach us. It's our job to welcome and invite them into our lives, even if we don't want to or understand why.

"People come into your life for a reason, a season or a lifetime. When you figure out which one it is, you will know what to do for each person."

Unknown

God has shown me that the quality of the special friendships that I have in my life is a reflection of just how much he loves me. All of our relationships can serve as a mirror to show us our own character and personality traits–the good and the bad. We can see ourselves reflected back through others in a way that we can't see by ourselves.

Do you get triggered by certain people? Is your reaction to them out of proportion to what they've done or said? Before you too quickly cut them out of your life, put up walls, or attack them, ask God what he wants you to learn about yourself. Where are you wounded? What buttons are being pushed? What are you believing? All relationships can be your teacher and a difficult relationship can be your greatest gift.

BUFFY

Dogs read our energy. When my sweet Buffy would "cop an attitude," I'd say, "Hey, what's your problem?" But then I'd realize that Buffy was communicating to me that my lousy attitude was the problem. I was the one who needed an attitude adjustment.

Pastor Kay Michaelis

You may also wonder why you are stuck in or have to go through a particular situation, but take a closer look at the potential lessons in that situation. You can trust that God is working through your situation to improve things on your behalf (Romans 8: 28).

What qualities or traits is God developing or refining in you through this situation? Like a good gardner, God prunes us so that we will bear more fruit (John 15: 2). What fruit are you bearing? What fruit do you need more of? Patience, perseverance, faith, better boundaries, compassion? God is not random. If you ask him, he'll show you. Ask him, "Lord, what do you want me to know about this situation?"

I never would have thought to get a dog to help me heal from my divorce. But God knows exactly what we need and the best way to meet that need; he is not limited by our conventional thinking (Isaiah 55:8-9). He knows where we might be defensive and he knows who or what has the best chance of getting through to us at any particular time. So, don't be surprised when he gets your attention in an unusual way.

Rescue Me

"He came to me as a rescue and I was supposed to be providing only a temporary home. I had just gone through a divorce and was feeling particularly self-focused. He took me out of me and got me hiking and caring about someone else again."

Chadia Webb

If We Could Talk to the Animals

My experience with Dallas was not the first time God used an animal for his purposes. The bible provides us with one example in the story of Balaam, a sorcerer whose greedy motives displeased the Lord. (Numbers 22).

Balaam was on his way to go see Balak, the Moabite king who wanted Balaam to curse the Israelites, when Balaam's donkey saw the angel of the Lord in the road. Afraid of the angel, the donkey turned off the road into a field. Despite being beaten by Balaam to make him keep going, the donkey would not continue on and eventually lay down. Finally, God caused the donkey to speak to Balaam. As a result of his interaction with the donkey, Balaam's spiritual eyes were opened and he repented.

In another situation, God also used ravens to tend to Elijah's physical needs by directing them to bring him bread and meat (1 Kings 17: 2-6). God cares about us and will sometimes use unconventional means to get our attention, meet our needs, show us his loving kindness, or bring us to a saving knowledge of Christ–whether it be a donkey, a raven, or a dog.

Go Directly to Jail

Surely, God would never use *prison* as a means to communicate his love for you? In Denver where I live, there is a dog training program at the Colorado Women's Correctional Facility (prison) that's called the Colorado Correctional Industries' Prison Trained K-9 Companion Program (PTKCP). Prison inmates take rescue dogs from "death row" (those who would otherwise be put down), and they socialize them and teach them manners and basic commands such as sit, stay, and heel. (https://www.coloradoci.com/serviceproviders/puppy/)

Enrolling your dog in PTKCP is a wonderful way to make sure your dog learns how to follow his master. But it also has additional benefits for the inmates. God is using dogs to transform these women's lives and heal their wounds right where they are–in prison.

Carol McKinley wrote an article about PTKCP called, *Dog Days at Denver Women's Correctional Facility*. She writes, "Most of them [the dogs] were brought in from area shelters where they were locked up, unwanted and out of chances. These women [inmates] know exactly how that feels." She quotes one inmate as saying, "They [the dogs] need to be shown how to live. In return, they show us how to live here." Another inmate states, "I don't think I would have made it in here without the dogs." www.correctionsone.com/corrections/arti cles/3166819-Dog-days-at-Denver-Womens-Correctional-Facility/

We shouldn't be surprised by a story like this. The bible tells us how Paul and Silas were in prison when God used their prayer and praise to loose the chains of all the prisoners and cause the prison guard to give his life to the Lord. He and his entire household were saved (Acts 16: 25-34).

In the same way that the dogs help the inmates and Paul's and Silas' imprisonment impacted the prison guard, perhaps God will use your metaphorical or literal imprisonment for your own or someone else's benefit.

What is God trying to tell you? Who is he using to reach you?

LESSON TWO

LISTEN

After my divorce, it was good to have a cuddly little companion like Dallas with me when I was alone in the house. Certain sounds would put me on edge, but I noticed that Dallas only barked when someone was at the door. Her little ears would perk up before I even knew someone was approaching the house. And then the doorbell would ring and she would run to the door barking. I didn't have to be afraid of every little sound I heard, because Dallas was listening for the ones that really mattered and I could be confident that she would respond accordingly.

Hearing is a passive activity; as long as your ears are working and a sound in your environment reaches a certain volume, you will hear it. In contrast, *listening* requires you to be alert, make the effort to pay attention, and be ready to respond. If you are listening, you are filtering out distractions and focusing in on a limited range of stimuli.

Have you ever been in a crowded room talking to the person in front of you, when from across the room, you heard someone say your name? Even though you were fully engrossed in the present conversation, somehow, you were still able to hear your name.

Psychologists call this the "Cocktail Party Effect." In the cacophony of ever-flowing sounds all around in your environment, it is possible to selectively attend to the one stimulus that is personally relevant or meaningful to you—for example, your name.

It put me at ease to know that Dallas would only bark when it really mattered. She was able to hear things that I couldn't, but she was not distracted by the random noises that caused me to be fearful. She *listened* for the sound of footsteps approaching the house—she was alert and ready to respond if necessary.

The Cocktail Party Effect reminds me of the Holy Spirit. God is always communicating with us, but he speaks in a gentle whisper (1Kings 19:12b). We will hear him if we will just open our hearts and *listen*. Listening begins with focusing in on the Holy Spirit and the sound of Jesus calling our name.

We need to become familiar with the sound of his voice so we will recognize it and listen when he is speaking to us. (John 10). Have you ever been in a situation that didn't work out well and afterwards you said, "Something told me not to do that"? Well, that *something* is the Holy Spirit.

Can You Hear Me Now?

In August of 2012, I resigned my job as a psychology professor after teaching for 19 years. Sometimes I think I should have stayed one more year just to make it an even twenty. But I knew very clearly that I had heard God say to leave and to leave NOW.

I shouldn't have been surprised. I had been wanting to quit for several years. I once said, "OK, God. I guess when you're ready, you'll let me leave." What God said in response was humbling: "Dear, I'm always ready. You're the one who's not." Silly me!

At the end of every spring semester—for 3 years—I begged God, "Please don't make me go back." The first year God said, "There's more for you to learn." The second year he said, "You complain too much." He showed me that I was like the children of Israel, grumbling and wandering in the desert. That year, I learned to be thankful and praise him regardless of my circumstances. The third year he said, "There's more for you to give" and he often reminded me, "It's not about the work. It's about the people at work."

It's funny how challenging times tend to bring us closer to God and motivate us to not just hear him, but to listen more intently. I was now *listening* diligently and seeking him for guidance, answers, and comfort because I so desperately wanted to leave my job. During these three years, I started to hear God speak in a whole new way.

In May of 2012, something shifted inside of me. I boldly told God, "I'm not going back. I don't know what your plan is, but this time, I'm not going back." I even started telling people that I was leaving my job. I had no clue how this was going to happen or what I would do next, but I was determined that come August, this time I wasn't going back.

Over the next 3 months, God started to very specifically speak to me about leaving my job. He spoke to me through what I was reading, the lyrics in a song, something a person would say to me, and different things I would see. But I still doubted that he was saying I could quit. I kept saying, "Lord, is this really you? I just need to know this is really you and I'll do it."

One Sunday afternoon after church, I was visiting with my friend, Joyce Riley at

Starbucks. Joyce is gifted in the "art of questioning." She knows just the right questions to ask to guide you to what you need to know.

In the midst of asking me several well-crafted questions about my desire to leave my job, Joyce stopped suddenly and said that God had just shown her the word "trust." She said it was written clearly in the air in front of my face in Times New Roman font, boldfaced and underlined like this: **<u>TRUST</u>**.

God knew the desires of my heart and he was finally allowing me to resign from my job as a psychology professor, but he also knew that I needed something tangible, specific, and clear. And so there it was—literally, the word TRUST. It doesn't get any clearer than that!

Doubting and still questioning, I prayed about what Joyce had seen. "God are you *really* telling me I can leave?" God answered, "What part of all of this does not add up to 'leave and leave now?'" How surprising that—after waiting for so many years to be released from this job—when the time finally came to leave, I didn't believe him and I was scared to go. I'm reminded of a series of experiments that were conducted by psychologist Martin Seligman.

In Seligman's experiments, a dog was placed in a partitioned box that was designed to deliver an electric shock on either side. The dog would receive a shock, and when he jumped over the partition to escape, he was shocked again on the other side. Every time he jumped to escape, he was shocked.

As you might guess, eventually, the dog learns to just lie there. Even if you could tell the dog, "I have now turned off the electricity, and you will never be shocked again. Go ahead and jump one more time," he still would not jump. He had learned to be helpless, to no longer jump, and to just lie there.

We are like Seligman's dogs. When we have experienced pain time and time again, it's as if we've been shocked into a state of passivity. We give up because we believe that whatever we do doesn't matter. God says he has turned off the electricity and it's safe to jump to the other side, but we don't believe him and we don't do what he tells us.

Go Ahead and Jump!

In the story of the invalid who had been lying at the pool of Bethesda, unable to get into the healing water, we see a similar picture of learned helplessness (John 5). Jesus asks the man if he wants to get well and he answers by giving excuses based on his previous experience: there is no one there to help him get in the water to be healed and everyone gets ahead of him in line. The man *never* actually answers "Yes, I want to get well!"

He's been sick for 38 years and he can't picture his life any different than it's ever been. He probably doesn't have much confidence that Jesus can heal him; hence, the excuses. Nevertheless, Jesus' response to him–if I may take poetic license à la Seligman–is basically, "Go ahead and jump!" (verse 8).

Can you imagine Jesus asking you the question that you have been waiting your whole life to hear? You feel nothing ever goes your way. You take one step forward and get knocked back two. You've been in a rut for years. You feel like your marriage is dead. Your children are in trouble. Your health is declining. Life has lost its excitement. Everyone else is getting ahead but you. And then Jesus asks you, "Do you want to _____ ?" [Fill in the blank: have your dream job, get married, make more money, lose weight...]?

Jesus is ready to give you the desires of your heart. What do you do? Do you make excuses for why you can't have the very thing you've been praying about and hoping for?

This is essentially what happened when I finally heard God say, "Leave and leave now." I couldn't believe I was hearing him correctly. Then, when he made it clear that I *was* hearing him, I felt afraid. I started making a list of all of the reasons I couldn't go and certainly not now.

How could I quit my job when I didn't have anything else lined up? How could I suddenly have exactly what I had been praying for when I didn't know what I would do next? I didn't believe what God was saying and I couldn't see how it was actually possible.

When you hear a word from God, it doesn't matter what you can see or not see. We should respond not based on what we *see*, but based on what we *hear* and what we *believe* about what we hear. (2 Corinthians 5:7; Romans 10:17).

When we position ourselves to *listen* to God, we are committing to wait patiently to hear what he has to say on a matter. And when we hear him say jump, we must believe we are able to jump, whether we can see it or not.

When Jesus told the man at Bethesda to get up, he was healed instantly! Had the man not *believed* he could walk, he would not have even tried to get up and walk. I believe that the healing miracle happened the moment the man believed–the moment that he *listened* to Jesus and committed to be alert, attentive, and ready to respond to whatever he heard him say to do.

Are you listening?

LESSON THREE

HEEL!

I was finally clear that God was saying it was time to leave my job. I was excited and at the same time terrified. And just like the invalid at Bethesda, I had my excuses.

Pastor Kay Michaelis, who is the head of the counseling department at my church always says that, "No, Lord" is an oxymoron. God is not truly Lord and Master if I tell him no.

Despite my fear and my excuses, I really did want to leave my job and I wanted to obey so I said, "Yes, Lord, I'll do it and I'll do it now."

When I arrived on campus to give notice, my heart was pounding and I felt light headed. My fantasy had always been that I would march into my boss' office and say, with a smug look on my face, "I just got my dream job somewhere else and I quit!" But when the time came, all I could do was humbly say, "I've lost my passion for working here and it's time for me to go."

I knew I was doing exactly what God told me to do, but in the moment I uttered those words, I was terrified and uncertain of what my future would bring. One thing I knew for certain, however, was that this one act of obedience would change my life.

After I quit, I thought to myself, "Oh boy, I am really taking a leap of faith." But God quickly showed me that it wasn't a leap, it was just one step. And *I* wasn't really taking the step; I was holding onto him and *he* was taking the step.

Over the next 4 months, God taught me how to position myself–to actively seek his voice, spend time with him every day, and abide in his presence. He also taught me that listening requires obedience and that it was not enough to obey; I had to obey quickly. In short, he was showing me how to follow him.

I Will Follow You

Just when I was becoming more comfortable with trusting God for whatever would come next, out of the blue, I was offered a temporary administrative position back at the college I had just left. Because God had been teaching me to listen to his voice, I said yes to the new job without all of the drama and doubt I experienced when I first heard him say leave earlier that year.

After a few days on the new job, however, I couldn't help but wonder if maybe I had made a mistake and I hadn't really heard God at all. Just a few months prior, he was telling me to leave, and now here I was back at the very place I had just left. When I asked him, "God, how did I end up back here?" he said, "You followed me here."

When a dog is well trained, his master doesn't actually have to say anything to get the dog to obey. The dog is so tuned in that he learns to respond to his master's non-verbal movements and subtle gestures. Like a woman dancing with her beloved, a dog learns to follow his master's lead.

"Heel" is a command given to a dog to walk close behind its owner; he should not be out in front or lagging too far behind and he certainly should not be following anyone else.

My Dallas would follow a squirrel or chase another dog and run after anyone who struck her fancy. While this may seem cute, a dog's failure to heel creates a safety issue for the dog and for others.

But it's not enough to just follow. One must learn *whom* to follow. Unfortunately, I didn't teach Dallas to follow *me*, her master–the one who would keep her safe from harm. If Dallas had learned how to heel, she might still be alive today.

Nelson

I once had a Bassett Hound who was the most frustrating dog I have ever had. When I was first divorced, Nelson—that was his name—became mine.

I moved to a different neighborhood and a new house. He was very difficult to keep in the yard and ran away several times. One day, I was taking a walk with him when this woman came up to me and said, "I know that dog. He is the dog that got in bed with me."

Shocked, I asked her what she was talking about. She told me that the day before, she was napping and she felt this cold nose on her face. Well, it seems that Nelson had escaped my yard and saw no problem going into her house through the screen door and getting right in bed with her!

He seemed very happy to see her again.

Donna Westmoreland

Count the Cost

The Gospel of Matthew gives accounts of a teacher of the law who has heard of Jesus and promises to follow him wherever he goes, of a disciple whose father has died, and of the disciples who follow Jesus into his boat. In all three cases, Jesus implies or directly explains that following him comes at a cost. In order to follow, they might have to give up a place to live, they might not have time to mourn lost loved ones, and they might have to give up their comfort and weather a storm instead (Matthew 8: 19-25).

Matthew also tells another story about a wealthy young man who asks Jesus what he can do to have eternal life. Jesus tells him that in order to have treasure in heaven (eternal life) he must sell his possessions and give everything to the poor. The young man is unwilling to give up his great wealth and walks away from Jesus. (Matthew 19: 16-22).

Many of us–like the teacher of the law and the wealthy young man–have a heart to follow God, but we also realize that following comes at a cost. You must give up your independence, autonomy, going where you want to go, and doing what you want to do. (You can read more about this in my book, *Do Something Different...For a Change*). But the good news is that following Jesus gives you a great reward (Matthew 19: 27-30). When we stay close to God and abide in him, we will have what we desire and produce good results (John 15: 7-8).

BAM!

I have a 6 year old lab/husky mix dog. I got stuck with her because I allowed my middle school daughter to talk us into getting another dog when we already had two—a male and a female. The other two dogs are gone and now it's just Jade, whom we've had since she was 3 months old.

The older dogs did not treat Jade well. They would not let her in the dog house and they nipped at her and shunned her. The female played with Jade sometimes, but not always.

On the positive side, however, the other dogs helped keep Jade in line. When we told them to do something, Jade went along with the program.

Over the years, Jade learned some good and bad behaviors from the other dogs. When they were no longer with us, Jade got a bit wild. She would not listen, she ran around the neighborhood, and when we would call her, she took her time coming to us or did not come at all. She would not stay out of the street and would bark at people. She was hard to handle and just gave us fits.

One day she got out in front of the house, doing what she always did—not listening or obeying our commands or instructions. Since my children were out there, I went back in the house and left her out front. Next thing I knew, I heard some commotion coming from the front of the house. My children came in to tell me, "Mom, your dog got hit by a truck!"

I wasn't surprised. I came out front and as I did, I saw Jade coming out from under a large, white truck. The truck had hit her and she had been pinned under it. She was lucky she didn't get pinned under a tire.

She was so frightened that she just took off running down the street with her tail between her legs, and then she disappeared in the neighborhood.

We spent the rest of the evening looking for her and calling her. We never found her. I thought she was injured and couldn't make it home or that she had gotten lost. We weren't sure what had happened.

Three days later, I was awakened by some scratching at our back fence. I got up and went out to see what it was, and lo and behold, there was Jade, wagging her tail, happy to see me with only a slight scratch on one of her legs.

Ever since Jade was hit by the truck, she has become the sweetest, most obedient dog I have owned. She has grown to trust me and know that I will take care of her, feed her, love her, and protect her.

Being hit by the truck was the best thing that ever happened to her. She is well-mannered now. She will not leave my side when I take her for a walk. She listens very well.

Jade will obey me even if others are trying to tell her to do something else, or if she wants to go and do something I don't want her to do. She will stop and follow my commands. But Jade will not follow a stranger's voice whom she doesn't know. If she is unfamiliar with them, doesn't know them, or hasn't spent time with them long enough to get to know them, she doesn't trust them.

My dog's behavior is not that much different than any of us when it comes to our relationship with God. Just like Jade, we run off on our own and do our own thing and then BAM! We get ourselves hit. Maybe we get pregnant/get someone else pregnant, we get fired from a job, we get a DUI, or someone else gets hurt. We steal some money, we cheat, we lie, we hate, we hurt, we deceive. We want what we want…and then BAM!

Anita Kelley

Take (Care of) Me, I'm Yours

When a dog is domesticated, he lives in his master's house and he eats his master's food. When he is sick, his master will take him to the vet. When he is dirty, his master will bathe him.

A domesticated dog even knows his master will pick up his poop and clean up behind him, especially if he poops somewhere he shouldn't. On the way home from a walk one lovely Saturday afternoon, Dallas actually rolled herself in dog poop and had poop all over her fur! Well, guess whose responsibility it was to clean her up?

When a dog is obedient and submits to live in a human's house and stay on a human's leash, the human is now his master and is consequently responsible for taking care of him. A master who doesn't take care of his dog can even be charged with cruelty to animals. But a dog who disobeys his master, doesn't stay on his leash, and runs off, is now on his own. His master cannot care for him or protect him.

When you submit to God's authority and Lordship over you life, it is now his responsibility to take care of you, to provide for you, to guide you, and to protect you. You don't have to do anything but follow him, submit to him, and love him, and you'll be cared for. You're his responsibility.

As I've embarked on my journey of self-employment (which God has told me to call *God*-employment), I've had to remind myself that I'm his responsibility. I have to stay focused on the sound of his voice, know that he is leading me, and obey. When I do this, I can trust that I'll have everything I need.

When we allow God to truly be our shepherd, to lead us and guide us, we'll never be in want (Psalm 23).

Run With the Big Dogs

Have you ever seen a little dog who doesn't seem to get it that he is little? The smallest dogs tend to be the yappiest of all. Experts call this "small dog syndrome"–

small dogs who believe they are the human's pack leader. The remedy for small dog syndrome is to train the dog to submit and surrender to his master's leadership.

Dogs with small dog syndrome have it backwards; they really are *not* the human's pack leader. But what I love about little dogs with small dog syndrome is that they *believe* they are bigger than they really are. You can't tell a small dog that he is not large and in charge.

God wants you to be bold in the face of opposition. You're with your master and he won't let anything happen to you. Stand up tall, hold your head up high, and bark like you're bigger than you really are because your master is bigger than any big dog that may try to intimidate you. He's given you power and authority to run with the big dogs. You are strong and capable and always have the victory through Christ (Philippians 4:13; Romans 8: 37).

Do What We Came to Do

When I first got Dallas, I was off from work for the summer. I wasn't in any particular hurry to do anything or to go anywhere, so I would take Dallas on long, leisurely walks. We would start out down the street where I lived, turn left at the corner, walk past the field at the middle school, walk all the way around the school, circle back to the field, and sometimes walk around in the field before heading back home.

Once summer was over and I had to go back to work, except for the weekends, I usually just took Dallas down to the corner and back. Our purpose was not to enjoy a leisurely walk, but simply to let her go to the bathroom as quickly as possible. Often, we'd almost be home and Dallas would still not have gone to the bathroom. I'd tell her, "Dallas, it's time to hurry up and do your business; we're almost home."

Dallas didn't seem to understand that on the days when I had to get to work or it was getting dark out, we had to do what we came to do. The walk had an intended purpose and a limited amount of time. The only way to accomplish our purpose was to stay focused.

Each one of us has a purpose and a destiny. God has plans for us (Jeremiah 29: 11) and often God's plans are time-sensitive—"for such a time as this" (Esther 4:14). God may open a window of opportunity for only a limited period of time, and if we miss it, we often miss out.

God has mercy and grace for us when we delay and miss the mark, but the opportunity may not come back around for a while or it may be harder to obtain the next time.

Delayed obedience is still disobedience. Dallas got out of the yard and was struck by a car and killed simply because she delayed her obedience. Had she obeyed immediately when I told her to stop and come, she would not have been hurt. Doing what God tells us right when he tells us to do it is just as important as doing the thing itself.

Bottom line, God wants to keep us safe, provide for our needs, and draw us closer to him. If we love him, we'll obey him (John 14:15). We'll do what he wants us to do, go where he wants us to go, and give what he wants us to give.

God doesn't like having us on a short leash. He doesn't like having us on a leash at all. He wants us to *want* to stay close to him and go where he goes. Just let him lead, and you follow. Don't run off and get hit by a car. Don't lag behind and get your neck yanked. Just heel.

Who or what are you following?

LESSON FOUR

STOP AND SMELL THE ROSES

Have you ever gobbled down a meal without really tasting your food or hurried your child through a conversation because you were running late? We miss so many beautiful moments in life when we rush through our day and don't "stop and smell the roses."

The bible tells us that we can see and understand God's power and divine nature through his creation. (Romans 1: 20). Wouldn't it be horrible to miss God because you didn't take time to admire, delight in, and enjoy his creation or savor the little things in life?

Maybe you've heard the saying, "Yesterday is history. Tomorrow is a mystery. Today is a gift. That's why it's called the present." The bible tells us not to worry about tomorrow. (Matthew 6:34). We have to have faith that God will take care of tomorrow so that we can enjoy today. We can be so focused on where we are going next and everything else that is going on, that we miss where we are right now.

I remember when I was teaching my children how to drive. I was out with my daughter one day and I observed that she was concentrating so much on where she was trying to drive next that she wasn't paying attention to where we currently were and what was happening around us. If you are looking too far out ahead of yourself, you will miss the things that are right in front of you.

Enough for the Present Moment

Have you ever driven on a dark highway with no street lights? You can only see a few feet in front of you. On a trip from Virginia back to our home in Colorado, I had just gotten behind the wheel for my turn to drive when my (now former) husband and I encountered a terrible rain storm. Visibility was practically zero and I was too afraid to continue driving.

He said he would drive and seemed to have no trouble seeing. I told him, "I'm impressed that you can see so much better than me." He responded, "I can't see very far either, but as long as I don't go too fast, the headlights illuminate the road right in front of me and I trust that the road will guide me."

I realized that I was too afraid to drive because I insisted on seeing more than just a few feet ahead of me. I wasn't comfortable not being able to see everything that was down the road.

We have to accept that we won't always be able to see everything that is down the road of life, either. We won't always know the outcome or where God is taking us and we won't always have information on all the variables involved in our situation. But what we do have is the present moment and what it possesses.

The present moment is where we find God. We have to trust that even though we can only see what's right in front of us, everything will be okay if we just keep going, slowly but surely.

Dallas taught me to stop and smell the roses and to be fully present in the moment. Time seemed to stand still for Dallas when she had a bone. I became mesmerized whenever I watched her with one. She stayed focused for hours, chewing zealously and undistracted until the bone was gone.

On those days when she didn't have a bone, Dallas often found a sunny spot and quietly lay down. She was unaware of anything other than what was right in front of her and that was enough for the present moment.

My Daily Bread

During my time of unemployment and subsequent *God*-employment, I developed a deeper understanding of what it means for God to truly be my daily bread–my manna. Manna is our provision for *today*.

When we are in the desert, God sends us manna each day. It may not be the tastiest gourmet meal we've ever eaten, but it will *sustain* us; it is *enough* for today.

God gave the children of Israel specific instructions for them to follow regarding the manna he sent. (Exodus 16). When they disobeyed those instructions and attempted to collect more manna than they needed for the day, the manna spoiled and they lost their daily provision.

God uses manna to also teach us the connection between *obedience* and *provision*. If you move out of God's will and disobey what he has already told you, you might still have *your* provision–what *you've* stored up or can provide for *yourself*–but you will miss out on *his* provision. God steps in and does what we cannot do for ourselves. But first we have to get to the end our ourselves and stop doing it in our own strength.

We fully experience life and all God has to offer when we live in the present moment–when we stop and smell the roses. We can't go back in time and we certainly cannot go forward into the future. We only have this moment right now....and then it's gone.

There is a man in Great Britain named Clive Wearing. Clive lost his short term memory after a bout with encephalitis. It damaged the part of his brain that holds his short term memory and carries it over to long term memory. Clive can remember his past–that he has a wife, he has children, he is a musician–but he cannot remember any new memories that have occurred since his illness.

This impairment in his memory also hinders his ability to anticipate the future because he has no memory of what just happened to link him to what could happen next. Clive cannot remember his immediate past and he cannot anticipate the future; he is very present moment aware because that is all he has.

To fully embrace the present moment requires us to be very still. It is in our stillness that we know God is God (Psalm 46:10a). Not only can I sit still and know he is God, *he* sits still, holds me in his arms, and listens to me. I can release all of my troubles and give them to him.

While crying out to God the other day about some concerns that I was facing, I heard him very clearly say, "Just come and be with me. That's where your peace is. That's where your provision is. That's where your joy is. Just come and be with me." It's comforting to know there is nothing I have to do or say. Just stop and be still.

God wants us to delight in his creation and rest in Him. Sit still in a sunny spot and contemplate his goodness, grace, love, and mercy. And what happens when we stop and smell the roses and sit still and know that God is God? Our only appropriate response is praise (Romans 12:1).

Jump and Dance!

Because Clive Wearing has no short term memory, whenever his wife walks into the room, Clive responds as if it is the first time he has seen her all day, even if she just stepped out of the room minutes ago and is now returning. His eyes light up, he kisses her, and he embraces her with joy.

Have you ever seen someone's eyes light up when you walked into a room? If you have a dog, of course you have! Dallas taught me what it feels like to be appreciated and loved unconditionally. Just like Clive, Dallas would jump and dance every time I came into the room, even if I was there only just 5 minutes before.

Dallas reminded me that I can jump and dance in God's presence and that God loves me unconditionally. As a matter of fact, God promises that he never leaves me so I can celebrate every moment that I'm with him.

Thinking about Dallas reminds me to slow down, stop and smell the roses, and never miss an opportunity to jump and dance in God's presence.

When is the last time you really danced?

LESSON FIVE

NEVER ABANDONED

Because of the harsh economic and political conditions that used to exist in Romania, many Romanian children were abandoned and sent to orphanages. Due to the sheer number of infants in these orphanages, the babies lived in appalling conditions and experienced very little human contact with caregivers. It was rare that the babies were held during feedings, burped, cuddled, or spoken to.

It is well established that newborns who receive inadequate amounts of human contact will literally fail to grow and can even die. This phenomenon is called, "Failure to Thrive Syndrome." Many Romanian orphans failed to grow or reach normal developmental milestones, and many developed disabilities and abnormal behavior.

When these babies were adopted by American families, their new parents found some of them to be extremely aggressive. The parents who already had other biological children reported that some of these adopted children were so aggressive that they were physically attacking their new siblings.

In some cases, the American parents sought to cancel the adoptions and send these children back to Romania. It's hard to imagine someone giving back an adopted child, but there were certainly days when I felt like un-adopting Dallas.

One of those days occurred soon after bringing Dallas home. I noticed blood coming out of her bottom. I thought she had hurt herself and so I took her to the vet. The vet promptly informed me that Dallas was in heat! The vet then instructed me to buy doggie diapers for Dallas (they have a little hole for the dog's tail to poke through) so that blood wouldn't drip all over my house.

Oh my, what had I gotten myself into?! I had impulsively adopted a dog who was having a period! I'm ashamed to admit that the thought did cross my mind to drop her off at a shelter somewhere and not look back.

He Won't Rub My Nose In It

Dallas got in the habit of running off and hiding under the couch when I tried to put her in her crate. On one particular Monday morning, I left Dallas out of her crate and home alone all day because chasing after her would have made me late for work. I figured that everything would be fine and so I went off to work.

Well, everything wasn't fine. When I got home, I discovered that she had chewed through an electric cord (that thankfully, was not plugged in) and she pooped and peed on the floor. Not sure what else to do, I put her nose close to the mess, rolled up a newspaper, and firmly spanked her bottom with it, saying, "Dallas, no!"

On several other occasions, Dallas pooped and peed on my basement carpet. I was so angry. Again, I put her nose close to the mess, rolled up a newspaper, and firmly spanked her bottom, saying, "Dallas, no!"

Opie

When Opie was a puppy, he would chew on my glasses, garden gloves, or a shoe. When I would scold him, he would confidently look up at me bewildered, as if to say, "What? Isn't this what I'm supposed to do? I'm a puppy after all."

Pastor Kay Michaelis

I'm so glad that God doesn't treat me the way I treated Dallas. God wants me to know that no matter what I do wrong, he won't roll up a newspaper, spank my bottom, and rub my nose in it. And he'll always wash me clean.

God wants me to learn, but he won't condemn me and he would never un-adopt me if I don't behave myself or if I "have an accident." And when I've made a mess for the fifth time in four days, he won't tire of me and feel like giving me away.

Bengee

Let me tell you about Bengee. Bengee was a Pekingese. I got him as a puppy. He was my best friend. We had such a bond, I referred to him as my son.

Around the age of 9, he lost sight in one eye. A year later he lost sight in the other. He had a problem with his back at an early age, and as he got older it began to affect his hips and he began to lose the ability to walk. With all of his health problems, he was difficult to care for.

When I traveled, it was hard to leave him in a kennel for more than 3 days. The only other person that could handle him was my mom, and she lives in Florida. On more than one occasion, he flew to Florida with me and I left him with my mom before I went on vacation. I then flew back to Florida, picked him up, and then flew back home to New York. (He had as many frequent flyer miles as I did).

It was around 2007 that Bengee's hips really started getting bad. He was already completely blind by this time. His hips were so bad that I had to carry him from time to time when we went out because he would just get tired.

I loved this dog so much, I did everything I could for him. I even took him to Connecticut to have him fitted for a doggie wheelchair. After spending a nice piece of change to have it made, he didn't like it, but that was OK, because I would do anything for him to make him comfortable. I found a wagon that I fixed up and when we went out, I would put him in his wagon. People thought it was cute, but they didn't realize that it was a necessity.

In the early part of 2008, I started to think about what might be best for him. He was in a lot of pain, so I thought about putting him down. But every time I thought about it I would cry, so I would just put it out of my head and continue to care for him as best as I could.

In March 2008, I gave my life to Christ. Soon after that, I found myself sitting on the floor crying, telling God that I couldn't do this alone anymore. Caring for Bengee was taking a toll on me physically—carrying him up and down the stairs and in and out of the house several times a day— and financially, as he had many medical bills.

Not a week later, I was in church and it was as if my pastor was speaking directly to me. I don't remember anything else he said except for this:

"When your parents get old, you don't put them in a home, you take care of them. When your dogs' hips give out, you don't get rid of them, you take care of them."

Right then and there, I knew that it was my responsibility to take care of him for as long as he could stand it. And I did that for another 5 months, until the pain was just too much for him to bear. At that point, I knew I had done all that I could to take care of him. Even though it hurt me to put him down, I was at peace because I knew that I was doing the right thing by not letting him suffer anymore. Keeping him alive to keep me happy was causing him to suffer and I couldn't continue to do that.

Bengee loved pizza. So the day that I had decided to put him down, I came home early from work and we had pizza together and took pictures.

Regina and Bengee

A year after he died, I just wasn't ready for another dog. I had so much love for Bengee that I didn't think that I could love another dog like I loved him. I did want another pet, though, as I missed the companionship, so I settled for a cat. (I guess my thinking was that it was a different species, so it would be OK). Well, now I have Gizmo, and my love for him is much like the love I had for Bengee.

Pets, no mater what kind, can give you unconditional love if you let them.

Regina Joyner

It doesn't matter who we are; God loves us in spite of all of our shortcomings and challenges. And though it is difficult to comprehend, his love for others doesn't diminish his love for me.

Pick Me! Pick Me!

Pastor Kay has another dog named, Opie—a dog with really long legs that look like they were made for a much bigger dog. I was in a small group that met at Pastor Kay's house for a 6-week study called, "Not a Fan." Over the course of these six weeks, we learned how to truly become a follower of Christ.

Every week, Opie greeted us at the door as we each arrived. He would pace around the room, testing out everyone's lap, and then pick one person's lap to stretch out his long legs in for the rest of the evening. He would let me pet him or sneak him a piece of my snack, but he never stayed with me.

Maybe I took Opie's rejection personally or perhaps he just reminded me a little bit of Dallas, but I longed for Opie to come and sit with me. "Pick me, Opie. Love me," I would silently plead, but Opie never did.

And then it happened. One evening, as the 6-week study was coming to a close, Opie finally picked me! He jumped up onto the couch next to me and then sat in my lap most of the night. I was so happy and just hugged him and pet him for as long as he would let me.

I was waiting all of that time with so much love and affection to share with Opie. If only he would have picked me sooner.

Opie and I

God showed me that the way Opie was with me is how I can be with God; God is always whispering, "Pick me. Love me."

Just as I was longing for Opie to pick me and sit in my lap, so too, God is longing for me to pick him, sit in his lap, and let him love on me.

Opie tried everyone else first before he picked me. And sadly, I am often the same way. I don't always turn to God as my first thought. I might try to solve a problem on my own or pick up the phone and call a friend before I think to pray and ask God to show me what he thinks about the situation or what he wants me to do. God wants to be my first option rather than my last resort.

In contrast, I think back on how Dallas treated me when I first met her. Immediately, Dallas scurried past everyone else and jumped up into my lap and lay down. It was as if she sensed my broken heart and wanted to comfort me. Remember, I had just gotten divorced the day before and had driven 13 hours to get a little respite from my emotional pain.

Dallas was just the cutest little thing—she was so small and so light in my lap—and such a comfort to me during this difficult time. She demanded nothing from me but to love her and be loved in return.

Recently, I was crying about a disappointment and God gave me a picture of Dallas in my lap. He showed me that my burdens can feel as light as Dallas felt in my lap if I would just let him carry them for me (Matthew 11: 30).

When Jacquie needed someone to adopt Dallas, I couldn't say no to that cute little face. I didn't know at the time that choosing Dallas would allow God to teach me so much about myself and his love for me. I can't help but wonder now, "Did I choose her or did she choose me?"

I Once Was Lost, But Now I'm Found

Over the course of my marriage and prior to divorcing, we had grown cold and distant from each other. Ultimately, my divorce felt like a rejection of who I was as a woman and a wife. A wife blossoms in the adoration of a loving, attentive husband and a part of her withers and dies when that is absent. Being in a marriage where you feel unloved and unwanted is very painful for a woman. And so, to have Dallas choose me, sit with me, and love me was the beginning of my healing.

Mitzi

Mitzi, a rescue dog, was able to tell me of her abusive history by her behavior. She was afraid of everything. She never barked. She would crawl when a man came in the room.

Apparently, she was a kennel dog who got beaten whenever she barked. She was so used to being abused and criticized that she became discouraged.

It's the same way with us. We so want to be and do and become what our parents or spouse want, but we are too afraid to try because we don't want to be criticized and experience their disappointment in us.

Until Mitzi felt safe, she wouldn't come out. Most rescue dogs have issues because they've been neglected and abandoned. I was amazed how encouragement would quickly draw her out. When I said, "Come," even if she just leaned in a little bit, I would get all excited over it and praise her efforts. She eventually came out and just blossomed.

I also tried to make it safe for her—I was there for her, I was covering her, always aware of her needs. She could relax and feel safe. I just let her be her. I didn't put her on a program to try to change her.

I just consistently tried to draw her out to be the dog she was created to be. I praised and rewarded her for her slightest effort. She eventually came out of her shell.

She was just so fabulous. Absolutely the best dog I ever had.

Pastor Kay Michaelis

In Hot Pursuit

We may feel that we are the ones pursuing God. It's true that if you seek God with everything you've got, you will find him (Jeremiah 29: 13). But God also pursues us and gives his all for us even before we actually know him and surrender our lives to him (Romans 5:8). As much as we may run away from God in any particular situation or season of our lives, he is always pursuing us like the "hound of heaven," and by any means necessary.

I intuitively sensed that Dallas' unconditional love would be just what I needed to feel redeemed and to restore my broken heart and so I brought her home with me. We had both been abandoned, and God so lovingly and strategically arranged for me to drive all those miles, not only to rescue this abandoned dog, but for her to rescue me.

Dallas taught me that God truly loves me and will never leave me. Even when it looks like I've been hopelessly abandoned, he'll send a kinsman redeemer (Ruth 3) who will travel many miles to take me in, care for me, and restore me. When I'm lost, he'll leave everyone else to come and find me (Matthew 18: 12). He loves me simply because to him, I'm just the sweetest thing in the world.

Are you feeling loved?

EPILOGUE

After Dallas died, I was reminded of a scene at the end of the movie, "The Prince of Tides." Nick Nolte's character is reflecting with deep fondness on his sister's psychiatrist, Dr. Lowenstein, played by Barbara Streisand. He spent a great deal of time confiding in her and sharing his deepest secrets with her.

Subsequently, their relationship and her influence had a profound effect on him. Where he had been cold and emotionally distant, her ability to listen and accept him–dirty secrets and all–brought him back to life. At the end of the movie, as he drives home with the top down on his convertible, he says:

As I cross the bridge that will take me home, I feel the words building inside me. These words come to me in a whisper. I say them as prayer, as regret, as praise, I say: "Lowenstein, Lowenstein."

As I walked through my empty house, soon after my beloved little companion was gone from this world, I felt these words building inside me. These words came to me in a whisper: "Dallas. Dallas."

I now realize it was the Lord speaking to me through the memory of my sweet little Dallas. Showing his loving kindness towards me. Embracing me. Comforting me. Calling me to him.

"Peggy. Peggy. You're just the sweetest thing in the world to Me."

DOGGIE OBITUARIES
AND CONDOLENCES

Cole

Cole has lived with us to teach us these important life lessons:

Patience & Perseverance: Go slow and wait on those less able to catch up. We are all doing the best we can.

Commitment & Discipline: Each day we consistently provide care, walks and treats. It builds security and confidence in those we care for.

Forgiveness: No matter what, Cole wags his tail, even on his bad days.

Raising Children: Walk alongside, play with them, and be their best buddy...until they're all grown up and move on.

*Unconditional Love: I will stay with my mom
until she knows she is worthy of being loved.*

*Cole came to me to show me my biggest lesson...
I am worthy of love.*

*And one day he will teach us the lesson of death
Even the sadness of separation, we let go ...*

*It is a peaceful rest
A green pasture
In the loving arms of Jesus
Cole will run and play again.*

*Because his lessons will live in our hearts
forever,
Cole will never die.*

Denise Materre

*Written 9/24/09 11:19 am
Cole made his transition 9/25/09 12:45pm*

Tank Dogg Lehman

The Dog, the Dane, the Dizzle was born May 22, 2002, in Bloomfield, Indiana and adopted by Jesse Lehman 6 weeks later. Tank was one of the Greatest of all the Great Danes and adored by everyone he encountered.

To know the gentle giant was to love him. Known as a golf course dog, Tank went to work everyday with Jesse at courses all over the country. Tank has resided in 4 states: Indiana, Wisconsin, Illinois, and Colorado. He was very well traveled!

He was also quite the personality, as he has been recognized across the radio airwaves of Chicago and Denver. Although he was a celebrity, he never let it go to his head! But being a philanthropist at heart, he did use his status to help other dogs. For the past two years, he walked in Denver's Mutts & Models, a runway fashion show that benefits pets less fortunate than himself. Unfortunately, Tank missed walking the runway by just 5 days this year.

Tank was a fighter having survived past the average Dane life expectancy by 3 years. But cancer took over Tank's body and his health quickly deteriorated.

Tank passed away peacefully on the morning of May 7, 2012, with his doting owners and very best friend, Jesse by his side. Tank joins his sister Baci "The Mastiff" Doering in Doggie Heaven. He will forever be missed.

R.I.P., Tank!

Erica Cobb

Peg,

I am so sorry you lost Dallas! You were just saying on Saturday how she has blessed your life. It looks like Dallas served a great purpose in your life. Sometimes we don't understand why things happen (or sometimes the timing), but God knows. I know you will find comfort in knowing that Dallas helped you through a difficult time in your life.

Take Care,

Mia

Oh, Peg.

I was sorry to learn that you lost your dog, and in such a tragic way. She was obviously the family member you needed, at the time you needed her. She requested so little, but brought you so much. Thank you for sharing the lessons you learned from such an inspiring four-legged wonder.

She REALLY was cute!

Love and God Bless,

Michele

Peg,

I'm so sorry to hear about Dallas. I know what it's like to lose a pet/friend/confidante and it leaves a big painful hole. It's heartwarming to hear Dallas' story, though, as it is one of love and hope. Her life had ups and downs and you were one of her blessings as much as she was yours. It's uplifting to know that God put the two of you together to help each other. Your article is excellent. I'd like to forward it to some friends at church, but I wanted to ask you first, because you might want to publish it!

Aleah, Bailey the dog, and I are all sitting here in a moment of silence thinking of you and Dallas. (Well, it's hard to tell exactly what Bailey is thinking of, but I pet him and told him about it.)

Thinking of you.

Melissa

Hi Mommy,

I'm really sad about Dallas. Why did God take away something that brought people so much joy? It doesn't seem fair. I miss her a lot. I wish she didn't have to get hit by a car. I hope it didn't hurt. I wish I didn't have to see her lying there on the road or hear the thump the car made. That's all I can think about now. I can't really focus. I keep crying in the middle of my homework. I miss her so much. It's not fair that she has to die, when she made us so happy.

Ali

Oh, my goodness, this just breaks my heart. I'm SO sorry, Peggy. It seems impossible after we just exchanged photos of and talked about our beloved companions.

I also love what you've written here—it's so true and made me cry. Dallas was precious.

Love,

L.

Hi Peggy:

I am sorry to hear about Dallas. You know that there is a reason, season, and purpose for everything, and it looks as if Dallas was in your lives for a reason. I hope that you continue to consider all of the beautiful joys that she brought and the lessons learned. Also, thank you for passing those lessons on. You should put it in a little booklet with Dallas' picture.

Love you,

Marian

Hi Peggy,

I am so sorry to hear about Dallas.

Thank you for your words of inspiration that encouraged me today. It is not unusual that God will teach us in ways we had not imagined. We just need to be still and stay in fellowship with Him.

Continue to hold on to His unchanging hand.

Blessings,

Jolianne

Peggy and children,

I am so saddened by the loss of your sweet Dallas—please know that God does not make mistakes, and Dallas was loved by you, Ali, and RJ. Please submit your wonderful essay about Dallas to a magazine—what a wonderful way to remember her.

On Monday, I gave my students a quote before I had them write a short paragraph—here is that quote:

"An animal's eyes have the power to speak a great language." - Martin Buber.

Dallas said what she had to say to you and now she is off to speak to others.

In peace,

Tilloretta

Dear Peg,

I'm so sad to hear this news....

I was with you at Panera Bread, and with Irene, when you told us about your trip from Texas to Denver with Dallas in your lap.

Your poem sure makes me think of the actions that God wants from us. Wow, you sure pay attention to detail. I have actually seen similar things done by dogs, but don't think I would have ever been able to put them in writing with such detail and beauty.

I'm praying tonight to the Lord our God, to give you peace in your heart, and to keep sweet Dallas' good moments in your memory forever.

Much love,

Luz

Peggy-

I'm sorry about the loss of Dallas. God brought her into your life for the right season and took her away for a reason that we don't always understand but was the right thing for now. I will lift you up in prayer and ask for healing of your sorrowful heart. Dallas is looking down thanking you for being such a wonderful master.

Much love from Texas,

Leland

Oh sweetie... I'm soooo sorry about Dallas...

Your essay is lovely and you're right, God uses many ways to speak to us. We just have to be aware and open for the messages...

What a sweet picture. You brought her joy as well.... you saved each other.

Love,

Irene

LESSONS I LEARNED FROM MY DOG DALLAS

(Original essay that I wrote a few months after I adopted Dallas. I emailed it to friends the day after Dallas died).

1)   "Heel!" God doesn't like having me on a short leash. He doesn't like having me on a leash at all. He wants me to want to stay close to him and stay in step and go where he goes. Let him lead, and I follow. Don't run off and get hit by a car. Don't lag behind and get my neck yanked. Just heel.

2)   Bark at the big dogs. God wants me to be bold in the face of my enemies because I'm with my master. Stand up tall, hold my head up, and bark like I'm bigger than I really am, because my master is bigger than any big dog that may try to intimidate me. I can be bold because I know my master won't let anything happen to me. I have power and authority to bark at the big dogs.

3) Jump and dance whenever I see Him. Jump and dance and squeal with delight when I usher in his presence. Even if I just saw him 5 minutes ago, jump and dance and squeal with delight again as if it's the first time all day.

4) Stop and smell the flowers. Don't rush through my day and miss an opportunity to smell something good, say hello to a new friend across the street, or chase a butterfly. Savor the little things he's put at my level for my enjoyment.

5) Be still. Sit still for long periods in a sunny spot and contemplate his goodness, grace, love, and mercy. God wants me to be still and know he is God. But when he calls me to go out and play, God wants me to jump, dance, and squeal with delight at yet another opportunity to be with my master. And don't forget to chase the squirrels while I'm out. Play hard then rest hard.

6) Do what I came to do. If we take a walk, and we're almost home, it's time to hurry up and do my business before we get back home. There are nice things to enjoy along the way, but the walk has an intended purpose, and it must be accomplished in the appointed time.

7) He won't rub my nose in it. When I "have an accident," God wants me to know he won't roll up a newspaper, spank my bottom, and rub my nose in it. He'll clean up after me. He wants me to learn, but he won't condemn me. And when I've peed on the floor for the fifth time in four days, he won't get tired of me and feel like giving me away.

8) Never Abandoned. God wants me to know he loves me and will never leave me. Even when it looks like I've been hopelessly abandoned, he'll send a kinsman redeemer who will travel many miles to take me in, care for me, and restore me. When I'm lost, he'll leave the 99 to come find me. He loves me simply because to Him, I'm just the cutest little thing in the world.

ABOUT THE AUTHOR

Dr. Peggy Mitchell Norwood is a mental health consultant, former psychology professor, and ordained minister. She earned her Bachelor's degree in Psychology from Brown University, her M.Ed. and Ph.D. in Clinical Psychology from the University of Virginia, and she is ordained as a teacher through Global Change Network, USA.

Believing that all good psychology is GOD psychology, Peggy's passion is to share effective psychological strategies based on biblical principles to help people to *live well*. Living well means more than just getting by; it consists of mental, emotional, physical, and spiritual healing that allows us to walk in freedom and wholeness every day. Peggy believes that with Jesus Christ, the proper knowledge, and the right tools, we can all live well.

She encourages all of her clients to be not just hearers, but doers of the word and believes if you want something different, you must *do* something different.

Peggy is also the author of *Do Something Different...For a Change: An Insider's Guide to What Your Therapist Knows (But May Not Tell You)*. She is currently writing the next book in her *Do Something Different* series.

For more information, to order books, or to share your doggie tales, contact:

info@drpegonline.com
www.DrPegOnline.com